THE BOOK OF
GARNISHES

For Lauren
and the
kitchen at
1206 Boeton St.

May 12, 1996 !

X. Man

THE BOOK OF

GARNISHES

JUNE BUDGEN

Photography by
PER ERICSON

HPBooks

ANOTHER BEST SELLING VOLUME FROM HPBooks

Published by HPBooks, a division of Price Stern Sloan, Inc.
11150 Olympic Boulevard, Los Angeles, California 90064
ISBN: 0-89586-480-0
Library of Congress Card Number: 86-81041
20 19 18 17 16 15 14 13 12 11

By arrangement with Salamander Books Ltd. and Merehurst Press, London.

Editors: Susan Tomnay, Chris Fayers
Designers: Susan Kinealy, Roger Daniels, Richard Slater, Stuart Willard
Food stylist: June Budgen
Photographer: Per Ericson
Typeset by Lineage
Color separation by Fotographics Ltd., London-Hong Kong
Printed in Belgium by Proost International Book Production

CONTENTS

INTRODUCTION

Three vital senses are aroused when a magnificent meal is produced. The first is sight, followed by the aroma and then the taste. When a dish is beautifully garnished it shows that love and care has gone into its preparation.

A garnish may be as simple as chopped fresh herbs, fried croutons or a berry fruit with a leaf, or quite elaborate like chocolate curls or a flower made from thinly sliced citrus fruits.

I've divided the book into three main parts: garnishes for savory dishes, garnishes made with fruit, and decorations for sweet dishes. Very few utensils are needed to make these garnishes, those that I have used are shown on pages 8 and 9. The only indispensable piece of equipment is a good sharp knife.

Garnishes that look complicated, like the turnip chrysanthemum on the cover, are in fact quite simply made by following the step-by-step instructions. They're fun to make too, and something the whole family will enjoy.

UTENSILS

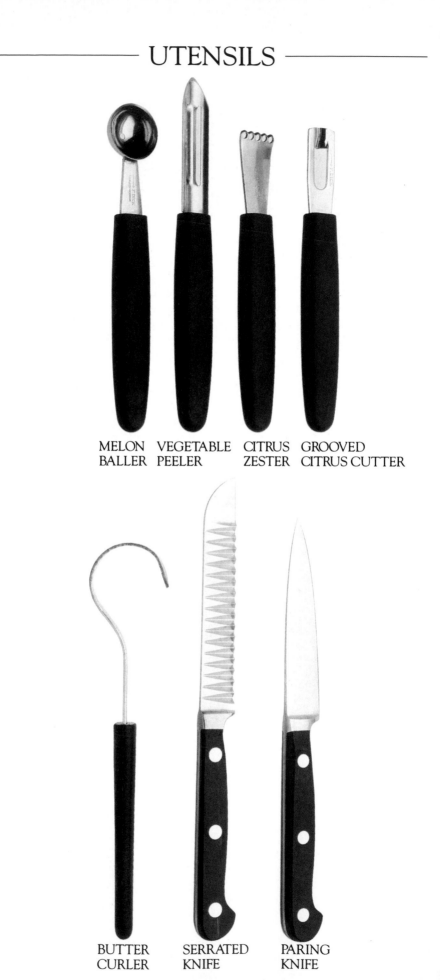

MELON   VEGETABLE   CITRUS   GROOVED
BALLER   PEELER   ZESTER   CITRUS CUTTER

BUTTER   SERRATED   PARING
CURLER   KNIFE   KNIFE

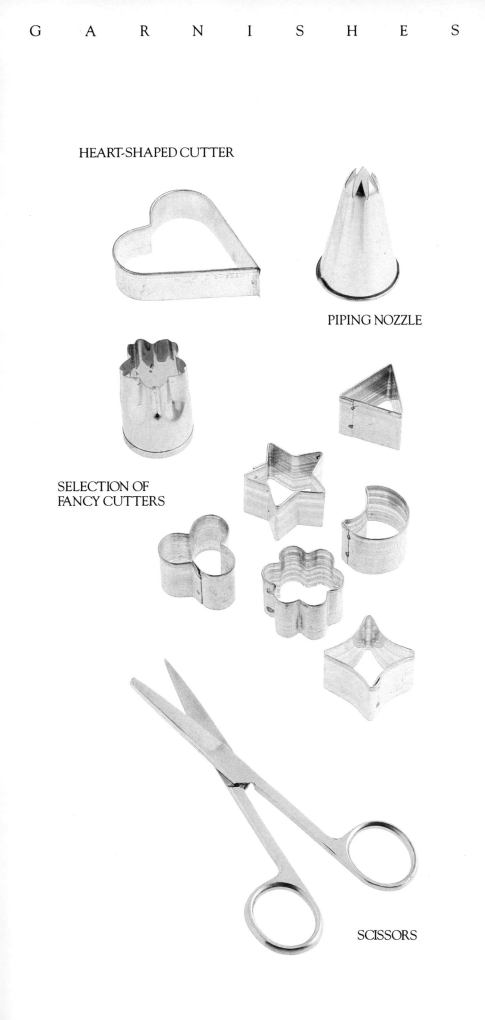

HEART-SHAPED CUTTER

PIPING NOZZLE

SELECTION OF
FANCY CUTTERS

SCISSORS

——— LEMON BUTTERFLIES ———

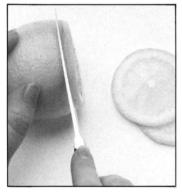

Choose firm lemons that have few seeds. Cut into thin slices with a very sharp knife; remove seeds. Limes and oranges can be cut the same way. Use to garnish fish dishes or to surround platters of food.

Cut a V-shaped wedge from the lemon slice. Turn lemon around and cut another wedge, making this one larger than the first. Discard the cut-out pieces. Place 2 fine strips of red chili pepper or bell pepper to represent the feelers.

Alternatively, the butterfly can be made by cutting the lemon slice into halves and reversing the halves so the curved peel is on the inside. Place the chili "feelers" in the center. Or omit the chili and replace with a strip of angelica or orange peel and use to decorate desserts.

CHILI WILD FLOWERS

Chili flowers are usually served with a dish that has chili in it, indicating to the diner that the dish is hot. Use small chilies or trim ends from the longer chilies, keeping the stem end for this garnish.

Rinse chilies in cold water and remove the seeds. Rinse hands in cold water as the chili can irritate fingers or wear rubber gloves. Avoid touching your face. Use a small pair of scissors and cut around the chili to form petals, taking care not to cut all the way to the stem.

Make several chili flowers in the same way and drop into a bowl of cold water. Store in the refrigerator until they open out. Alternatively, a simple chili garnish is made by cutting chilies crosswise into slices and using several together to top a dish.

RADISH ROSES

Wash round red radishes, leaving a small leaf attached, if desired. Trim away the root and scrape away any small hairy roots from the end. To make the tulip-shaped flower, hold the radish in one hand and cut a thin petal of skin starting at the root end and leaving the base of the petal attached. Repeat all the way round making 5 petals.

Radish roses are made by cutting off the root leaving a circle of white. Cut out a petal of skin in the side of the radish, leaving it attached at the base. Make 3 or 4 more petals, spacing them evenly around the radish.

Drop the radish roses into a bowl of iced water and leave to open out. When making many radish roses, use a large bowl so there is room for them to open out.

Radish roses are used for decorating cold meats, salads and sandwiches and as a crudité for dips.

AVOCADO FANS

Starting at the pointed tip of a ripe avocado, cut through the skin and flesh until the seed is reached. Run the knife all the way around the avocado. Holding the avocado in both hands, twist and separate the halves. Cut the half lengthwise into 2.

Remove the seed and cut the remaining avocado half the same way. Make 3 to 4 lengthwise cuts in the avocado quarters about three-quarters of the way through, leaving the top quarter uncut.

Peel away the skin and fan out the slices as they are placed on the plate. Avocados need to be prepared as needed because they will discolor. Use for salads or first-course dishes.

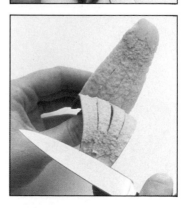

LEEK BOWS

An unusual garnish that looks good on top of tomato salads, with fresh aspara-gus salad or use to surround cold sliced meats. Use the green tops of fresh leeks and drop into a bowl of boiling water to soften. Drain when cool.

Take 1 strip and split into 2 if it is wide. Curl the strip of leek around to form one side of the bow. Do the same with an-other strip of the leek top and place them side by side on the serving platter. Trim ends neatly.

Using another piece of softened leek, wrap it around the center of the 2 loops to complete the bow shape. Cut away any unwanted ends with scissors.

CARROT BUNDLES

Choose tender, young carrots; peel thinly. Cut off a thin lengthwise slice from each carrot. This makes the carrot stable when slicing thinly. Cut carrots into finger lengths. Place carrot cut-side down; cut into thin lengthwise slices.

Stack 3 or 4 carrot slices on top of one another; cut into fine matchstick strips. Drop into boiling water to blanch 30 seconds. This brightens the color. If serving carrots cold, refresh under cold running water.

For the ties, use the green tops of green onions. Pour boiling water over to soften; drain and rinse under cold water. Cut the green onion into narrow strips. Take a bundle of the carrots and tie with the green onion. Serve hot as an accompanying vegetable or cold for salads and party platters.

CUCUMBER TWISTS

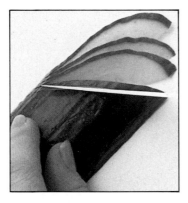

Use long tender cucumbers which have few seeds. Halve the cucumber lengthwise. Slice off end with a diagonal cut. Keeping the same angle, make paper-thin slices, taking care not to cut all the way through. Make 7 or 9 slices in each group.

Hold the cucumber piece skin-side down and cut the skin away from the flesh, starting at the end where the skin was not sliced. Cut along the skin until there is about ½ inch left. Leave this part uncut.

Turn the cucumber over and bend every second slice back to the joined end, leaving the alternate slices straight. Place in a large bowl of iced water and leave for several hours or longer. The skin will lift away from the flesh making a spectacular garnish which can be used to decorate platters of cold meats and seafood.

TOMATO WILD ROSES

It is important to use firm tomatoes for this garnish which can be used to decorate most meat platters and oriental dishes. Halve the tomato straight down the center from the stem to the base. Lay the tomato half cut-side down, and slice across into very thin slices using a fine-bladed, sharp knife.

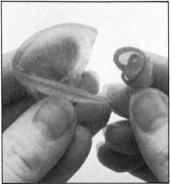

Roll one slice into a cone, then surround with another slice of the tomato. From this point it is easier to shape the flower upside down, so place the top of the flower face down on a flat surface.

Arrange the next petal, skin-side down, around the cone of the tomato; then add another, overlapping the slices. Continue until the rose is the desired size. For a rosebud, about 5 slices of tomato is enough. Place an egg slice or wide spatula under the flower and turn over, reshaping gently with fingers if necessary.

POTATO BASKETS

A special frying basket is needed for making these nests of fried potato. A larger basket can be made using 2 Chinese wire frying spoons. Peel potatoes and slice thinly. Arrange overlapping slices in a frying basket which has been dipped in oil to prevent sticking.

Fold the top of the basket over and clip into position. Heat a pan of oil for deep-frying. When hot, lower the potato basket into the oil. When a light golden color, lift the basket out of the oil. Drain, remove the potato basket and prepare more.

Before serving, reheat the oil and lower the potato baskets, one or two at a time, into the oil with tongs. Cook until golden. Drain and serve as an accompaniment to a meal, filled if desired with vegetables or as a starter with deep-fried shellfish.

—— TOMATO SUNFLOWERS ——

Place a small cherry tomato stem-side down. Cut the skin of the tomato across the base and down the sides leaving ¼ inch of skin uncut at the stem end. Turn the tomato and make another cut.

Make 2 more cross cuts in the same manner so there are 8 even segments in the tomato. The cherry tomato sun-flower can be used to garnish hot or cold dishes, salads and party dips.

Carefully peel the skin "petals" away from the tomato flesh, doing one petal at a time and cutting almost to the base. A few chopped chives or a pinch of chopped parsley can be placed in the center of the flower.

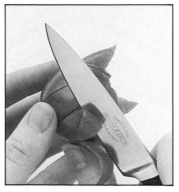

BEET CURLS

Beet stems make an unusual garnish. Formed into curls, they look very attractive piled in the center of a food platter. Cut stem from beet and trim to about 6-inch pieces, discarding the leafy tops. Make a series of angled cuts down the stem, being careful not to cut right through.

Use a fine-bladed, sharp knife and carefully cut each stem lengthwise into thin strips, the thinner the strips the better they will curl. Cut at least 3 strips from each length of stem.

Drop the strips of stem into a bowl of iced water and leave to curl. If making lots of curls, use a large bowl so the strips can curl without tangling. Keep in water, in the refrigerator, until needed.

STUFFED EGGS

Place eggs in a small saucepan, pointed-end down and packed closely so they stand upright without rolling over. Cover with water; bring to a simmer and cook 10 to 12 minutes. Pour in cold water until eggs are cool, then peel and cut into halves.

If preparing ahead, keep egg whites in a bowl of water in the refrigerator. Push the yolks through a sieve and stir in enough mayonnaise to give a smooth piping consistency. Season with salt, pepper and a little prepared mustard to taste.

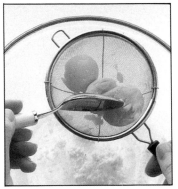

Fill a piping bag with the egg-yolk mixture and keep in the refrigerator until ready to serve. Drain the whites; slice a little from the base of each, if needed, so they sit flat. Pipe the yolk mixture into the cavity. Garnish with caviar.

CUCUMBER BOATS

Use tiny tender cucumbers for this garnish which makes an excellent hors d'oeuvre. Trim ends from cucumber; cut each vegetable into short pieces. Split each piece into 2.

Make a thin lengthwise slice parallel to the center, taking care not to cut right through the end. Leave about one-quarter of the slice still attached. Scoop out the seeds to form a hollow hull of the boat.

Fill the hull with red or black caviar and fold back the top slice to resemble a sail. Secure with a wooden pick. Use as a garnish for hot or cold seafood or as an appetizer.

LEMON BASKETS

Select a lemon with smooth skin, free from blemishes. Place the lemon on its side and cut halfway down the lemon, slightly off center. Start another cut of the same depth alongside leaving a piece in the center for the handle.

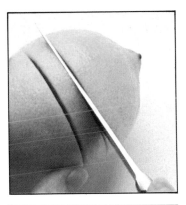

Make a horizontal cut from the stem to the first cut; lift out the wedge of lemon. Do the same with the other side; the basket is beginning to take shape. Limes and oranges may be prepared the same way.

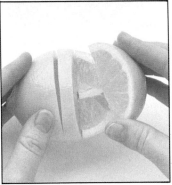

Cut away the flesh under the handle and scoop out the flesh in the base. Fill with greens or lemon wedges to accompany fish and chicken dishes or use to add color to food platters.

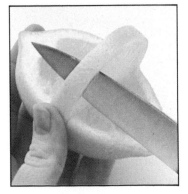

EDIBLE PEA PODS

Because of their bright green color and crisp delicate flavor, pea pods are a natural garnish. Added raw to salads, lightly cooked as a vegetable accompaniment or served as a crudité, they make the simplest meal sparkle. One way to prepare pea pods is to cut a triangular piece from the end of each pod so it has 2 peaks.

Another method is to cut the pods into julienne strips. These can be used raw in salads, added to soups just as they are being served, or mixed with strips of carrot or red pepper and heated gently to serve as an accompanying vegetable.

To enhance the color of pea pods, blanch them. To do so, bring a saucepan of water to a boil over high heat. Drop in the pea pods. Return to a boil; immediately plunge pea pods into iced water to chill.

LOBSTER BUTTERFLIES

An exotic garnish for serving with any lobster or crayfish dish. Once the meat has been removed from the lobster, cut the tail away from the shell using a heavy knife or scissors.

Cut crosswise through the center of the tail, chopping it into 2 pieces. Remove and discard the center section of the tail so each half of the lobster tail has 2 full sections. Trim away any meat and rough pieces of shell.

Flatten out each section of the tail, pressing with the palm of the hand. Arrange tail, butterfly-fashion, on the serving platter. Break ends from feelers and place on the tail so they form the body and feelers of the butterfly.

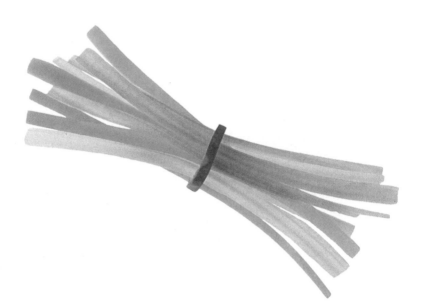

── JULIENNE OF VEGETABLES ──

Select vegetables such as carrot, celery and red bell pepper. Other suitable vegetables include parsnip, edible pea pods and turnip. Use to garnish main courses and for salads. Cut celery into finger lengths; then slice lengthwise into matchstick slices.

Cut the carrot the same way. Drop carrot and celery strips into a saucepan of boiling water; boil 1 minute. Drain. If the vegetables are to be served cold, refresh under running cold water. For hot garnish, season with a little salt and 1 teaspoon butter.

A few strips of red bell pepper add color to the julienne or a strip can be wrapped around the vegetables. To prepare the pepper, place under a hot broiler, skinside up, until the skin scorches and blisters. Scrape the skin away; cut flesh into thin strips.

——— DAIKON RADISH TOPS ———

The tops of the white daikon radish make an attractive garnish. Cut the tops into finger lengths and wash away any grit. Lay the length of stem flat and, holding the knife at an angle, make a cut in the stem slicing about halfway through. Continue making cuts along the stem at even intervals.

Slice the stem lengthwise into 2 or 3 pieces but leaving it attached at one end. Celery can be cut the same way but the thicker sticks of celery will need to be cut into 2 or 3 narrower strips before making the first cuts.

Drop the daikon tops into a bowl of iced water, leaving plenty of room for the stems to curl. Leave for several hours or overnight. Use as a garnish for salad platters or for dishes such as honeyed chicken wings or barbecued pork.

CROUTONS

Perhaps the best-known garnish of all. Piled into a bowl of hearty soup, it's no wonder croutons are so popular. Remove crusts from thickly sliced bread; cut bread into cubes. It is better to use day-old bread.

Heat ¼-inch oil in a frying pan. Add 2 tablespoons butter to give a good flavor. Heat until bubbling. Add a layer of bread cubes; cook until golden, stirring and turning constantly. Drain on paper towels.

Another bread garnish for soups is to slice French bread; then dry it out on a tray in one layer in a 250F to 300F (125C to 150C) oven until crisp. Halve a clove of unpeeled garlic and rub the cut side over the bread. Sprinkle with a few drops of olive oil.

MELBA TOAST

Using a serrated knife, remove the crust from a loaf of unsliced bread. It is easier to make melba toast with bread which is 1 or 2 days old. Cut the bread into chunks about 3 inches thick. Cut each chunk of bread diagonally into triangles.

Cut the triangles of bread across into thin slices. Place in one layer on several baking sheets. Bake in a 350F (180C) oven 15 minutes or until crisp and golden. Turn bread occasionally to color evenly. Cool and store in an airtight container.

Another way to make melba toast is to lightly toast thick slices of bread. While still hot, remove crust. Split each slice into two and then halve diagonally. Bake until crisp and golden. Serve melba toast with soups, pâtés and dips.

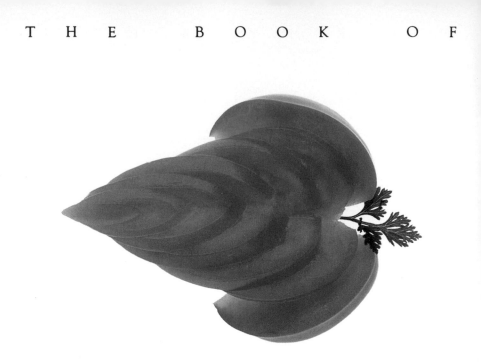

TOMATO WINGS

Halve a tomato lengthwise and place cut-side down on a board. Make a small diagonal cut into the center of the tomato; then make another cut in the opposite direction and lift out the wedge.

Continue to cut the tomato, following the lines of the first cut and remove each piece as it is cut until there are 2 wedges of the tomato left. Trim away the stem from the wedges.

Reshape the tomato half back into its original form. Gently move each tomato slice to separate and then open the bottom wedges to form wings. Use to garnish salad and cold-meat platters.

LEMON SWANS

Use a large lemon for the best effect. Oranges can also be cut the same way and make an attractive decoration for cakes and pies. The lemon is served mostly with seafood and fried dishes. Slice the lemon and cut each slice into 2.

Make a cut between the peel and the lemon to separate the peel. Cut almost to the end of the half slice, leaving a small section connected. For the best results, use a very sharp knife so the cut is clean.

Tuck the cut peel in towards the lemon slice to resemble a cup handle. This garnish looks striking when grouped, as above, or the lemon swans can be used singly. For drinks and punches, make a cut in the flesh of the fruit and place it on the rim of a glass.

ZUCCHINI TWISTS

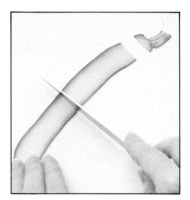

Using a vegetable peeler, slice zucchini into long slices. Place in a heatproof bowl; pour boiling water over, then drain. Refresh with cold water until zucchini is cool. This makes the vegetable pliable.

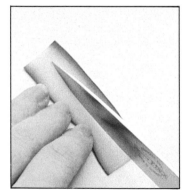

Trim away stem end and cut zucchini into halves or suitable lengths. Carrots may be sliced the same way and boiled 1 minute before being rinsed with cold water. Make a number of these twists to add to salads.

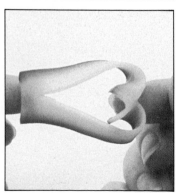

Make a lengthwise slit in the center of the piece of zucchini, being careful not to cut through the ends. Fold one end of the zucchini under and through the cut in the zucchini. The vegetable will twist naturally.

BEAN BUNDLES

Strips of dried gourd shavings, also called *kampyo*, are available in packets from Asian food stores. The strips are edible and look decorative when used to tie bundles of vegetables. First, soak gourd shavings in heavily salted water and knead well until pliable. The salt helps to soften the fibers. Wash well in plain water.

Drain gourd shavings; place in a small saucepan with a little water, a dash of soy sauce and a pinch of sugar. Simmer 10 minutes, then cool. Clean beans and remove strings, if any. Halve beans lengthwise, if large, and cut into even lengths.

Tie groups of beans into bundles, trimming off the ends of the gourd. Drop bean bundles into a large saucepan of boiling salted water; cook 10 minutes or until tender. Serve bean bundles hot as a vegetable accompaniment to meals.

──── HONEYCOMB SQUID ────

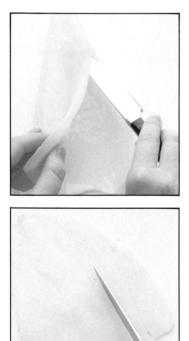

The method of crisscross cutting squid is basically to tenderize and to give the squid an attractive appearance. Remove the head from squid; wash the body well. Remove the ink sack, backbone and peel off any skin. Make a single cut down the body so it can be flattened out.

Open out the squid body and, using a very sharp knife, cut parallel lines down the squid keeping the lines close together. Be careful not to cut right through the flesh.

Make more cuts in the opposite direction to make a diamond pattern. Cut the squid into 3 or 4 pieces. Cook briefly in a shallow pan with a dash of water, a little soy sauce and a pinch of sugar. The squid will curl up when cooked.

Squid cooked this way can be served hot or cold as a starter to a meal, for picnics or in a seafood platter.

── TOMATO BUTTERFLIES ──

Use these attractive wedges of tomato individually for salads and to garnish many savory dishes or place 2 together to resemble butterflies. Choose ripe, red but firm tomatoes, cut into 8 even-sized wedges.

Peel the skin away from the flesh of the tomato wedge, starting at the base. Use a very sharp vegetable knife. Cut halfway along the wedge leaving the rest of the skin attached to the tomato.

Gently bend back the skin of each tomato wedge. Place 2 tomato wedges, skin-side together, and angle them to resemble a butterfly. This makes an effective border for salad platters.

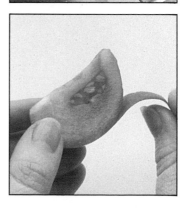

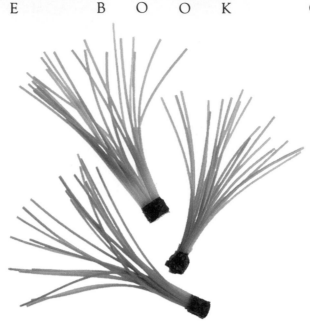

NOODLE BRUSHES

The fine wheat noodles from Japan called *somen noodles* are used to make these deep-fried brushes which are used to garnish fried foods. They are fun to make and pleasant to eat. Take about 15 sticks of the noodles from the bundle.

Break ends off the noodles, leaving a length of about 4 inches. Cut a strip of nori seaweed with scissors and wrap around the middle of each bundle of noodles. Moisten the end of the nori with egg white to adhere. Let stand for a few minutes for the seaweed to dry.

Cut through the middle of the nori so each bundle makes 2 brushes. The brushes can be prepared to this stage and left until ready to serve. Deep-fry in hot oil until golden, about 30 seconds. Drain. The noodles will spread open in the hot oil.

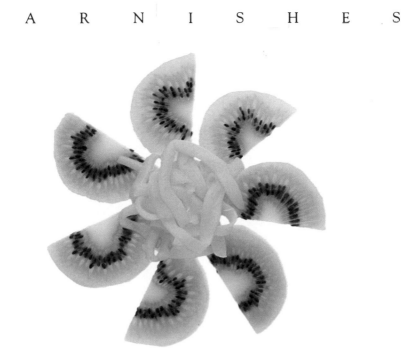

—— SQUID AND KIWI FRUIT ——

The delicate flavor of squid makes it a versatile partner to many foods. Use tender young squid. Remove the head from the body. Clean the body. Remove the ink sack, backbone and peel off any skin. Halve the body lengthwise and cut across into fine shreds.

Drop the squid into a pan of boiling water. As soon as the water returns to a boil, remove and drain. Rinse with cold water until cool. Overcooking squid will toughen it. Peel the kiwifruit; cut into halves lengthwise and slice across.

Mix 1 teaspoon light soy sauce with 1 tablespoon lemon juice and 1 tablespoon water. Stir in squid; season to taste with soy sauce. Arrange kiwifruit on a plate and top with squid. Serve as an appetizer or as a garnish to a cold seafood platter.

SPINACH MOLDS

These molded vegetables are an appetizing accompaniment to most meals and are also good eaten cold. Wash 1 large bunch of spinach, removing all the grit. Cut away the stems and put leaves into a saucepan with 3 tablespoons water. Cook 2 minutes and drain well.

Line small oiled molds with some of the leaves. Purée remaining spinach leaves in a food processor. Melt 2 tablespoons butter in a saucepan; add 2 tablespoons all-purpose flour. Cook 2 minutes, stirring constantly. Add 1 cup milk, stirring until sauce thickens.

Add sauce to the spinach in the food processor along with 3 eggs. Process until smooth and blended. Season to taste with salt and pepper. Spoon into lined molds. Place in a steaming basket; cook over simmering water 10 to 15 minutes or until set. Turn out and garnish with a few pine nuts, if desired.

——— WONTON PASTRIES ———

With scissors cut nori seaweed, available from Asian food stores, into squares the same size as wonton wrappers. Dampen the wonton wrapper with egg white and place the square of nori on top.

Fold the square of nori-coated pastry over, seaweed-side out, and adhere by brushing the edge with egg white. Make cuts with scissors along the rolled edge of the square, being careful not to snip all the way through.

Roll up, sealing the end with egg white. Deep-fry in hot oil until golden. Drain and use to garnish fried foods. Deep-fried parsley is another garnish for fried foods. Make sure the parsley is dry and clean. Drop a little at a time into hot oil; remove immediately and drain.

CARROT STARS

Cut young carrots into thick slices; then cut into shapes with a flower cutter. White daikon radishes or white turnip can be prepared in the same way and tinted with a few drops of food coloring diluted with water.

Make a cut from the center of the carrot shape to one of the indents in the edge, cutting almost through to the base of the carrot. Starting at the next petal, make a diagonal cut from the top to the bottom of the first cut. Remove the piece of carrot.

Repeat all the way around until 5 petals are carved in the same way. Drop carrot stars into a pan of boiling water; cook 1 minute. Drain and refresh with cold water. This heightens the color. Use for garnishing almost every savory dish or as a vegetable.

—— FLUTED MUSHROOMS ——

Select very fresh button mushrooms for this garnish. If necessary, wipe the caps with a damp cloth. Take the mushroom stem in one hand and, holding a sharp knife against the mushroom, make a curved cut around the mushroom, starting at the center of the cap.

Alongside the first cut, make a flatter cut so the piece of flesh will lift off giving a strong grooved flute. Continue around the mushroom. The trick in turning mushrooms is to press the mushroom firmly against the knife and not to put pressure on the knife.

Trim off stems level with the caps. Gently sauté the mushrooms in a little butter until tender. Serve hot to garnish almost any meat or chicken dish. The mushrooms look good when set in a line on top of dishes, such as creamed veal.

— TURNIP CHRYSANTHEMUMS —

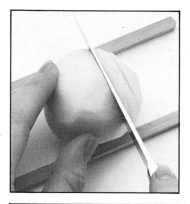

Peel a white turnip; place on a board with a wooden chopstick on each side of the turnip. Use a fine-bladed, very sharp knife to slice all the way along the turnip. The chopsticks prevent the knife from cutting through to the base of the turnip.

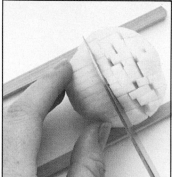

Give the turnip a half-turn and then, leaving the chopsticks in the same position, slice the turnip again crisscross style. Make sure that the knife cuts straight and not at an angle. Soak the cut turnip in a mixture of 1 tablespoon salt and 2 cups water to soften. Rinse well.

The turnip chrysanthemum may be colored by dropping into a bowl of cold water tinted with food coloring. Leave until the desired color is achieved; take out and gently move "petals" to give a realistic appearance. Use to garnish salad and meat platters and oriental dishes.

VEGETABLE SHREDS

Fine shreds of colorful vegetables set off many dishes like fried rice, curried meat, salads and soups. The green tops of fresh, crisp green onions will curl when a length is cut into fine shreds. If necessary, drop into cold water for a few seconds. Iced water will make the onion curl tightly.

Citrus peel, in this case lime, is cut with a zester to give appeal to desserts and some savory dishes adding a tangy flavor. Simply run the zester along the peel of the fruit. Alternatively, the peel can be cut thinly from the fruit, the white pith removed and the peel cut into fine shreds with a sharp knife.

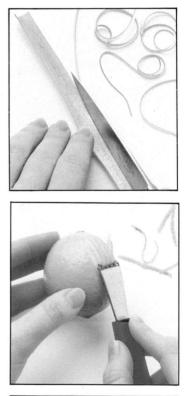

The finely shredded skin of tender cucumber added to grated white daikon radish is a refreshing color combination. Serve with fried foods or in salads. Use a citrus zester or grater. The Japanese vegetable shredder or mandolin is also good for shredding vegetables.

CITRUS TWISTS

An extremely simple and very effective way of displaying citrus fruits, such as limes, lemons and oranges. Slice the fruit thinly; place each slice flat and make a cut into the center of the slice, as shown.

Hold the slice of fruit in the fingers of both hands placed on each side of the cut; then twist in opposite directions. Two or three slices can be placed on top of one another and twisted together to give a double or triple effect.

This lemon and lime garnish is made by twisting a slice of lime as before. Take a slice of lemon and make a longer cut, past the center. Twist the lemon and place over the lime twist. Use for almost any dish, particularly seafood.

─── CUCUMBER LOOPS ───

Use the long, tender cucumbers that have very few seeds and a tender skin. Wash under cold water and trim off one end to a slight point. Cut around the cucumber, holding the knife at an angle so a coil is formed.

When 2 full coils have been completed, cut through the cucumber flesh to separate the coils from the cucumber. Continue cutting around the cucumber until there are sufficient coils for the garnish.

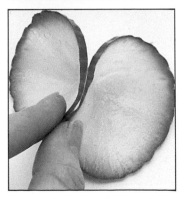

Take one end of the coil and curl it around to form a loop. Do the same with the other end. Use to garnish sliced cold meats or for a decorative border for egg and rice dishes or salads. A fresh cherry, when in season, can be placed in the loops.

——— DAIKON FLOWERS ———

This garnish is one which will take practice to perfect. The secret is to use a very sharp, fine-bladed knife and to have patience. Peel a white daikon radish. Cut off a piece 3 inches long. Holding the radish in one hand, start to cut a thin sheet of the radish, moving the blade in a sawing rhythm while turning the radish with the other hand.

When the sheet reaches 6 inches or more, cut away from the radish. Lay the sheet of radish on a flat surface and make parallel cuts along the sheet close together but not through the top and bottom edges, the same way a paper lantern is cut.

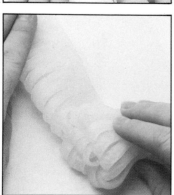

Fold the top edge over to meet the bottom edge and start rolling up the strip. Secure with a wooden pick. Color the flower, if desired, by soaking in water with a few drops of food coloring added. Use to garnish cold sliced meats, buffet platters, dips and Japanese meals.

—— BUTTERFLY SHRIMP ——

Shrimp prepared this way are used to garnish salads, food platters, seafood pâté, omelets or on top of thick cucumber slices for hors d'oeuvres. Peel the shrimp, leaving the tail intact. Make a cut along the back of each shrimp, and remove the vein.

Lay one shrimp on its side and, using a small sharp knife, slice through the back of the shrimp, making sure the tail and the flesh at the head end are not severed. Cut all the shrimp the same way.

Turn the shrimp over so the back of the shellfish is facing up, and open out gently to form a butterfly shape. It may be necessary to gently press the flesh to flatten it slightly. The tail will naturally curl over into place.

PICKLED GINGER ROSES

Pickled ginger, imported from Japan, is available from Asian food stores and is sometimes natural in color, pink or red. Buy the sliced ginger, not shredded. Open the packet and drain, reserving the juice to store the unused ginger in the refrigerator.

Take a slice of ginger and roll in your fingers to form a cylinder to make the center of the rose. The pickling juice that clings to the ginger provides moisture for the petals to adhere, needing no wooden picks.

Add petals to the rose, one at a time, crimping the ginger and gently rolling back the edge to give a realistic look. Squeeze the base of the rose so the flower holds together. In Japan, pickled ginger is served with sushi. It goes well with fried foods and fish.

SLICED AVOCADOS

A change from the usual halves of avocado, these slices look spectacular when a large platter of them is prepared, sprinkled with a little French dressing and freshly cracked black peppercorns. Halve the avocado by cutting all the way around through to the seed. Twist to separate, then pull apart.

Remove the seed and peel away the skin. Place the avocado, half cut-side down; slice crosswise along the length of the avocado, making the slices at even intervals. Slide a wide spatula under the avocado and place on a serving platter. Repeat with the other half.

Gently press the avocado so it spreads out; it will do this naturally. Our photograph shows the avocado half with a Lemon Camellia, see page 93 for Lime Camellia, and sage leaves.

── GREEN-ONION BRUSHES ──

Green-onion brushes are traditionally used to brush plum sauce onto the pancakes that accompany Peking Duck, the onion brushes being eaten also. Wash green onions; cut each into 3 or 4 pieces. Cut off the roots and discard most of the green tops.

Use a sharp vegetable knife and make a cut down the piece of onion, taking care not to cut all the way through so the brush will hold together. Turn the onion and make another cut at a right angle to the first, then continue making as many fine cuts as possible.

Put brushes into cold water 20 minutes or longer so they open slightly. The brushes may also be used in salads or for decorative borders or served with beef fondue, guests brushing their cooked beef with the selection of sauces using the green-onion brushes.

ONION WATERLILIES

Use the bulbous green onions or small white onions. Peel, wash and cut off the green tops. Cut a Van Dyke pattern, see page 86, or adjoining V-shapes around the onion, making sure the knife cuts through to the center.

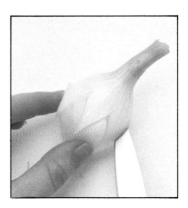

Separate the 2 halves by gently pulling apart; put into a bowl of iced water for several hours or overnight in the re-rigerator to allow the onions to open out. Onions will keep for several days in water in the refrigerator.

The onions may be left white or tinted with a few drops of food coloring added to the water. To achieve the two-toned effect, soak onions in lightly colored water; then dip into a very strong solution of the same color. Trim off the root and use onions to garnish food platters, particularly Eastern dishes.

——— CUCUMBER SPRINGS ———

Cucumber springs can be used to garnish platters of cold meats, and short lengths are fun in salads. Use small tender cucumbers that have very few seeds. Cut the cucumber into approximately 3-inch pieces, discarding the ends. Poke a wooden chopstick right through the center of the cucumber.

Holding a small sharp knife at a slight angle, make the first cut all the way through to the center of the cucumber until the knife hits the chopstick. Continue cutting around the cucumber turning the chopstick as the cucumber is being cut until the end is reached.

Remove the chopstick and pull the end of the cucumber gently so it forms a "spring". The ends may be joined to form a circle or the spring can be placed around a dish as a border. A slice of red radish placed between every second coil adds extra color.

—— RED-PEPPER TRIANGLES ——

Cut a piece from a red bell pepper; trim away some of the fleshy underside and remove any ribs. Carrots may be prepared in the same way by cutting into a long strip and boiling 1 minute. You can use lemon and orange peel too, cutting a thin slice of the peel using a vegetable peeler.

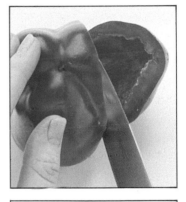

Cut the pepper into rectangular shapes 1 × ¾ inches. Make a cut along the longer side of the rectangle, one-third of the way in, and leave one end attached. Turn the piece of pepper around and make another cut parallel to the first and again not cutting all the way through.

Holding the 2 ends of the pepper, twist to form a triangle. Use in salads, with dips or to garnish cold meats. One triangle of lemon peel is often added to Japanese soups, giving fragrance, flavor and eye appeal to the soup.

BREAD ROLLS

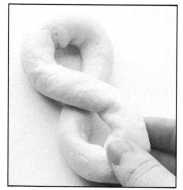

Bread Knots: Many shapes of bread rolls can be used for dinner rolls. Follow a favorite recipe or use packaged bread mix. Leave rise according to the instructions. For bread knots, roll a piece of dough to a strip ½-inch in diameter and 10 inches long. Gently tie a single knot, as shown; leave rise and bake as directed. If desired, brush with beaten egg and sprinkle with sesame seeds before baking.

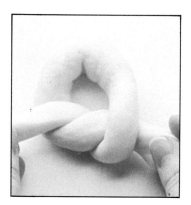

Figure-8 Rolls: Make a sausage of dough 10 inches long and 4-inch in diameter. Pinch the ends together forming a circle of dough. Lay the circle of dough flat; flip one edge over to form the figure 8. Leave rise on greased baking sheets and bake as directed.

Clover-Leaf Rolls: Pinch off small pieces of dough and form into 1-inch balls. Place 3 balls of dough close together in greased muffin cups, leave rise and bake as directed.

—————— BUTTER SHAPES ——————

Butter Balls: Take a 1 inch piece of chilled butter and roll between 2 wet butter paddles until a round shape is formed. Keep chilled and serve with bread or crackers. The butter balls may be rolled in cracked peppercorns or chopped parsley.

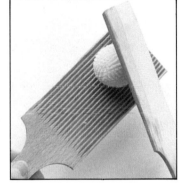

Butter Rolls: Pull a curved butter curler over a slab of chilled butter. Dip the butter curler into hot water before starting each roll. The slab of butter must be well chilled.

Herbed Butter: Mix chopped fresh herbs into room temperature butter; then chill until slightly firm. Form the butter into a roll; wrap in plastic wrap and chill until firm. Slice to serve with bread or crackers or use to top hot grilled steaks.

CARROT CURLS

Peel young tender carrots. Trim off the top stalk end. Use a vegetable peeler to cut into strips. If the carrot strips are too thick, they will not roll; some peelers cut finer than others.

Roll up the slices of carrot and place close together in an ice-cube tray. Put a chunk of carrot in the ice-cube tray to prevent the rolls from uncurling while more are made.

Pour water over the carrot rolls and place in the refrigerator for several hours or up to 2 days. The rolls are drained and used to garnish salads, dips or meat platters. The curls may be cut with scissors into finer strips for a lighter effect.

─────── BACON ROLLS ───────

Remove any rind from bacon slices. Choose bacon with a good pink color and well streaked with meat and fat. Cut each slice into 2 or 3 pieces; trim so they are an even width. Trimmings can be used for soups and stews.

Roll up each bacon slice and secure with wooden picks. Thread 3 or 4 rolls on a skewer. Bake in a pre-heated 400F (200C) oven in shallow dishes until golden and crisp. Alternatively, bacon may be grilled, turning frequently to color evenly.

Remove skewers and wooden picks from the bacon and serve hot. Bacon rolls accompany many dishes, such as roast or fried chicken or turkey and cream soups. They are delicious added to a freshly tossed salad.

—————— CUCUMBER PEAKS ——————

Cucumber peaks can be served as an hors d'oeuvre with a dipping sauce. Carrots can also be cut the same way. Use small tender cucumbers; wash and trim off the ends. Halve the cucumbers crosswise.

Lay a piece of cucumber on its side and insert a knife through the skin, past the center and through the skin on the other side. Make a slit, taking great care not to cut right through to the ends of the piece of cucumber.

For a zigzag effect, use a serrated knife for the next step. Sit the piece of cucumber upright with the slit facing you. Make a diagonal cut down one side of the cucumber. When the center cut is reached, turn completely over and repeat the diagonal cut on the other side. Gently ease the two apart.

RADISH FANS

Wash radishes well and remove leaves, keeping the smallest leaf attached for easier serving. Trim off the root end and make crosswise cuts along the radish taking care not to slice right through.

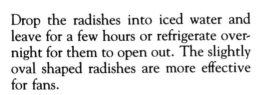

Drop the radishes into iced water and leave for a few hours or refrigerate overnight for them to open out. The slightly oval shaped radishes are more effective for fans.

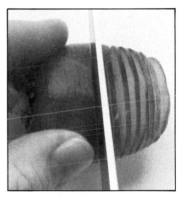

A simple and effective alternative is to halve the radish lengthwise and cut out a triangular-shaped piece, as shown. Radish garnishes are used extensively for salads and cold platters and to accompany dips. They also go well with fried foods.

──────── CARROT CACTI ────────

Peel young carrots and cut into halves if they are long. Drop into a saucepan of boiling water and simmer 5 minutes. Drain and rinse under cold running water until cool enough to handle. Using a citrus grooving tool, make a fluted pattern all the way around the carrot.

Trim one end of the carrot to a point resembling a pencil. Use a small sharp knife and, holding the carrot point down, thinly slice around the point of the carrot to form a coil. When 3 rounds are completed, cut the coil off and continue to make more coils in the same way.

Turn the ends of the coil in toward the center to give a three-flowered effect. Keep in water to prevent drying out until ready to use. Carrot cacti can garnish salads and meats and even decorate carrot cakes.

——— ZUCCHINI ASTERS ———

The zucchini must be cut very finely for this garnish. A Japanese kitchen cutter or mandolin is good, or a cheese slicer or vegetable peeler can be used to give a very thin lengthwise slice.

Using a sharp knife, make cuts along one edge of the zucchini slice, keeping the cuts close together but taking care not to cut all the way through. The zucchini slice at this stage resembles a comb.

Roll up the slice of zucchini and secure with a piece of wooden pick. Sit upright for the "petals" to open. If the zucchini breaks while rolling, the slice is not fine enough but it can be remedied by pouring boiling water over it, then refreshing in cold water.

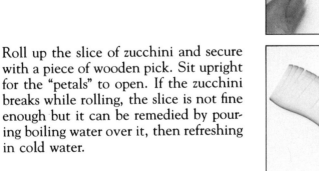

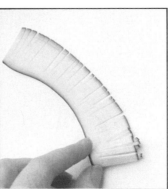

EGGPLANT WHISKS

Use tiny eggplants for this garnish, which is Japanese in origin but can be used for almost any dish, particularly fried foods. Score each eggplant lengthwise from the bottom leaving the top part attached.

Heat a pan of vegetable oil for deep-frying. Wipe the eggplant well with paper towels and drop into hot oil, a few at a time. Fry about 3 minutes. Lift out and drain on paper towels.

Fan out the eggplant by pressing with the blade of a small knife. Smaller whisks can be made the same way, first halving the eggplant lengthwise, then cutting into fine slices, leaving the top intact. Fry the same way.

PANCAKE SACKS

Make a batter with 3 eggs, 1 cup all-purpose flour and 1 cup milk; blend in a food processor. Use to make thin pancakes about 7 inches in diameter. Spoon a cold filling in the center of each pancake. Fillings can be creamed mushrooms, creamed spinach or diced blanched vegetables in a cream sauce.

Soak strips of dried gourd (kampyo) in heavily salted water and knead until pliable. Wash well in plain water. Bundle the pancake up over the filling and tie each into a sack with a piece of the gourd. If pancakes have been frozen, steam briefly before filling to avoid cracking.

Place the sacks in an oiled steaming basket. Set over a pan or wok of boiling water; cover and steam 10 minutes. Serve hot as a starter or as an accompaniment to grilled meat, chicken or fish.

—————— LOTUS FLOWERS ——————

Lotus root is available in cans from Asian food stores. It has a crisp texture and is a pleasant addition to salads. Lotus flowers can also be used to garnish food platters for buffets or added to casseroles and Chinese-style dishes. Drain the lotus root and slice thinly.

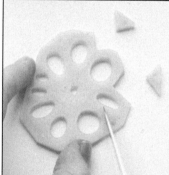

The slices of lotus root have a natural attractive pattern which can be enhanced by cutting out pieces between the outer holes and rounding off where needed. Use a small sharp knife for this.

Lotus slices may be dropped into a dressing of 2 tablespoons white vinegar, 1 tablespoon water and 1 teaspoon sugar. This salad goes well with fried foods or makes an interesting addition to other salads. A few drops of red food coloring may be added to give a pretty pink color.

RADISH SPINNERS

An easy garnish that can be used for salads and party food platters or to sit on top of stuffed eggs. Wash red radishes and trim off the root end. Cut radishes crosswise into thin slices.

Using a small sharp knife, make a notch in each slice, cutting from center to outside. The small, narrow variety of cucumber can be cut the same way for an alternative garnish.

Holding 1 slice of radish in each hand gently push 1 slice into the other at the notch so they connect to form a spinner. Repeat with more radish slices.

MERMAID TRESSES

Mermaid tresses are the shredded leaves of Chinese cabbage which have been deep-fried. They are used as a base for fried foods or to sprinkle over Chinese dishes to add color and texture. Wash the Chinese cabbage; dry well and cut away the stems. Use the stems for stir-fried dishes.

It is important that the leaves are thoroughly dry before cutting. Layer the leaves between sheets of paper towels and press firmly so the paper absorbs any moisture. Stack the leaves on top of one another and roll up. Cut into fine shreds.

Heat a small saucepan of vegetable oil for deep-frying. When hot, lower the shredded greens into the oil; leave for 3 seconds and scoop out immediately. Drain on paper towels. The cabbage will crisp as it cools.

PAPPADAM CUPS

Use the small round pappadams or cut large ones to a smaller circle with scissors. Heat a small saucepan with vegetable oil for deep-frying. The pappadams are cooked, one at a time and can be prepared 1 or 2 days before serving and stored in an airtight container. Place 1 pappadam in a small Chinese wire frying spoon.

Hold a pair of closed tongs in the center of the circle of pappadam and lower the frying spoon into the hot oil. The pappadam will curl up around the tongs forming a cup. Each pappadam takes only a few seconds to cook and should be pale golden in color.

Lift the pappadam above the oil; tilt to pour oil from the cup, then drain on paper towels. Just before serving, fill the pappadam cups with julienne of vegetables to accompany fried or grilled fish or fill with sliced tomato and cucumber for curries.

EGG GARNISHES

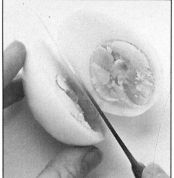

There are many uses for hard-cooked eggs when garnishing. The secret in cooking the eggs so the yolks are centered is to place the eggs close together so they can't roll around in a small saucepan. Cover with cold water; add a pinch of salt and bring to a boil. Cook exactly 10 minutes.

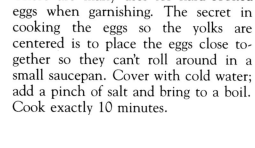

Pour off the hot water and rinse with plenty of fresh cold water until eggs are cool. This stops the cooking. Overcooking causes a green ring to form around the yolk. Eggs may be sliced or halved. Use a stainless-steel knife for cutting eggs.

The whites can be cut into fancy-shapes and used to garnish terrines, pâtés and legs of ham or other aspic-coated dishes. For the flower, arrange petal shapes of egg white, make a stalk from a chive or parsley stem and sieve the yolk for the center of the flower. Oregano was used for leaves.

ROYALE

Royale is the name given to a classic garnish for soups. It is a cooked savory custard which is cut into shapes and added to clear soups. Beat 3 eggs with ¼ cup beef or chicken broth or water and ¼ teaspoon salt. Use less salt if using already salted broth.

Use a fork or small whisk and stir to avoid bubbles forming on the top. Pour the custard through a sieve into a dish lined with waxed paper. Place in a steamer and press down the paper lining if it floats on the custard. Steam 15 minutes or until set.

Cool, lift out the custard with the paper lining and cut into fancy shapes using small cutters. The custard may be colored by adding cooked puréed spinach or tomato paste. Mix well into the eggs before steaming. An alternative way to cook is to bake in a preheated 300F (150C) oven until set.

SOUP GARNISHES

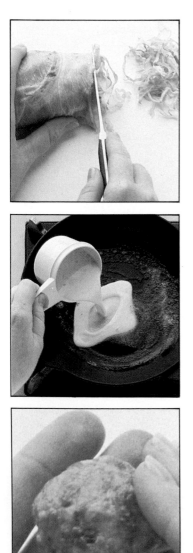

Chiffonade: There are many garnishes to complement soup, one being the classic Chiffonade. Use the well-washed outside leaves of lettuce, stack leaves on top of one another, roll up and shred finely. Add to clear soup, return to the boil and serve.

Shredded pancakes: Blend 1 tablespoon all-purpose flour with 1 egg and ½ cup milk to form a batter. Heat a greased pan and make thin pancakes. Stack 3 to 4 pancakes on top of one another, roll up and cut into slices. Add the shreds to clear soups and heat through just before serving.

Meat balls: These make a hearty soup. Mix 8 ounces ground beef or veal, 2 tablespoons finely chopped onion, ½ teaspoon salt, a dash of pepper, 2 eggs and ½ cup soft white breadcrumbs. Form into balls with wet hands. Drop into simmering water 10 minutes. Drain and add to clear soup.

SOUP DUMPLINGS

These dumplings can be steamed, boiled or deep-fried to serve with soup or as an hors d'oeuvre with a chili sauce for dipping. The filling can be meat, fish or vegetable. Buy wonton pastries and cut into circles with a round cutter.

Place a small spoonful of the filling in the center of each round. Brush the edge of each circle with some lightly beaten egg white and fold one side of the pastry over the filling to meet the other edge, pressing gently to seal.

Holding the 2 points in each hand, twist around to join, adhering with a little egg white. Cook the dumplings in deep hot oil until golden or drop into a saucepan of boiling water 10 minutes. Drain and serve.

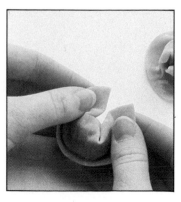

CARROT KNOTS

Choose young carrots that are not too short. Peel the carrots and cut lengthwise into very thin slices. Trim off the ends and cut slices into ½-inch wide strips. Drop into a saucepan of boiling water; cook 1 minute. Drain and rinse in cold water.

Cut the ends of the carrot strips at an angle. Make a loop of one of the carrot strips and hold in one hand. Holding another loop of carrot in the other hand, weave one loop through the other.

Keeping the 2 loops in the same position, feed the ends of one loop through its own loop, then gently pull both ends so the tie will knot. Use in salads or as a decorative border. Zucchini strips can be prepared in the same way, needing only to be dipped into boiling water to soften.

VEGETABLE TIES

Use a vegetable peeler to cut fine strips of zucchini and carrot. Use the skin of the zucchini also as it has good color. Pour boiling water over the strips of vegetables and let stand 1 minute; then drain. Blanching makes the vegetables pliable for tying in knots.

Cut the zucchini into narrow strips. Do likewise with the carrot. Other vegetables that can be prepared this way are edible pea pods and white turnip. Large white daikon radish looks colorful when prepared this way and tinted with beet juice.

Tie the strip of vegetable in a single knot and trim the ends, if desired. A pile of carrot and zucchini ties makes a fun salad drizzled with a lemony French dressing. Or heat in a little butter with cracked pepper for a hot vegetable dish.

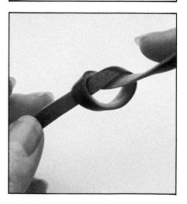

OMELET SHREDS

Omelet shreds are used to garnish soups, fried rice and noodle dishes, and in salads. Beat 3 eggs with salt and pepper to taste and 1 tablespoon cold water. Chopped herbs, such as parsley, chives or fresh coriander, may be added.

Heat a lightly greased frying pan; add enough egg to form a thin layer. When the underside is set, turn the omelet over for 10 seconds. Remove and cool. Make more omelets in the same way using the rest of the egg mixture.

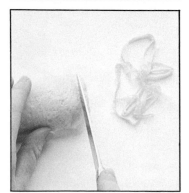

Stack the cooled omelets on top of one another, then roll up. Using a sharp knife, cut across into fine shreds. The omelet can also be cut into 1-inch squares.

———— SLIVERED ALMONDS ————

Slivered almonds are used to garnish savory or sweet dishes, such as poultry and ham salads, rice and poached fruit or for cakes. First, blanch the almonds by putting them into a pan of hot water. Bring to a boil, then drain and cool slightly. Squeeze each almond and the nut will pop out of its skin.

Use a very sharp knife or a safety razor blade kept for this purpose and split almonds, then cut each half into fine slivers, about 16 to each nut. Place on a baking sheet in a 300F (150C) oven 10 minutes to dry.

For toasted almonds, place the blanched and slivered nuts on a baking sheet in a 350F (180C) oven until golden, turning them occasionally to color evenly. Alternatively, the almond slivers may be fried in a little butter until golden. Use for savory dishes.

CUCUMBER BORDERS

A colorful garnish for bordering many dishes, such as shrimp, egg or meat platters. Use the tender-skinned cucumbers which have fewer seeds. Halve a cucumber lengthwise and place, cut-side down, on a surface. Make paper-thin slices across the cucumber, taking care not to cut all the way through.

When making the eighth slice, cut right through the cucumber so it is separated. Continue to slice the length of the cucumber in the same way. Repeat with the other half of the cucumber.

Fan out each group of sliced cucumber with fingers and place around the edge of a serving dish so it looks like a continuous border. See page 124 for photograph using the cucumber border.

CUCUMBER FANS

It is preferable to use small tender cucumbers. Pickled gherkins may be cut the same way. Use a sharp knife and halve the cucumber lengthwise. Then cut each half across to make 4 pieces. Scrape out the seeds with a teaspoon.

Place the cucumber, cut-side down, with the curved end facing you. Cut very fine strips along the cucumber, taking care not to slice right through the top end.

Sprinkle cucumbers with salt; let stand 20 minutes to soften. Gherkins don't need salting. Wash the cucumber to remove all the salt. Lay the cucumber flat and gently press with a knife so the slices will naturally fan out. Cucumber fans can be used to garnish almost any savory food.

──────── CARROT FREESIAS ────────

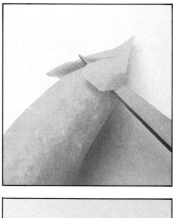

Choose young, tender carrots and peel thinly. Hold the carrot, pointed end down. Using a sharp knife, make a cut toward the point of the carrot to form a petal. Take care not to slice all the way through. Repeat cuts around the carrot to make a four-petalled flower.

Angle the knife slightly, then apply a little pressure to separate the flower from the carrot. For the first few flowers it may be necessary to ease every petal in this way, but after a little practice, the flowers will come away easily with a twist of the knife.

When the flower breaks away, continue to make more. A cluster of freesias, as shown above, makes an appealing garnish. To improve the color, drop carrot flowers into boiling water; boil 1 minute, then drain and rinse well under cold running water.

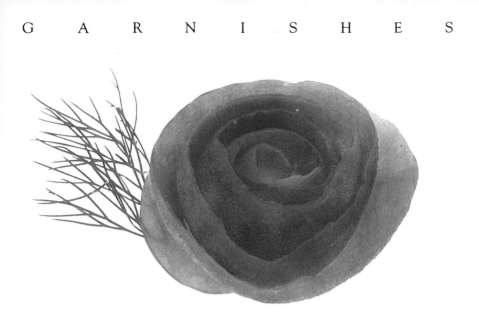

TOMATO ROSES

Starting at the base of the tomato, peel a thin strip all the way around the tomato, finishing at the stem end. The strip must be peeled thinly so it will roll evenly. Make sure your knife is sharp and the tomato is ripe but firm.

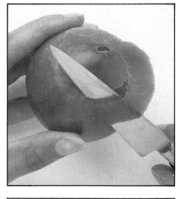

Place the strip of skin, flesh-side down, on a board. Beginning with the stem end of the strip, start rolling up the tomato skin to form a coil.

When almost all the skin has been rolled, sit the tomato flower on its base and curl the last piece of the tomato skin around to form the more open petals of the rose.

GREEN-ONION WHISKS

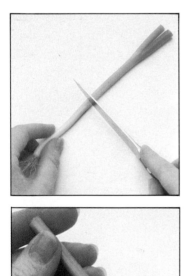

Wash green onions and trim off some of the green top. Cut off the white bulb where it starts to turn green. Keep the bulbs for cooking. Fresh crisp green onions will make the best garnishes.

Using a pair of small kitchen scissors, cut down the greenest part of the onion, stopping about halfway down. Continue to snip the onion into fine strips. Sometimes there are 2 branches of the green. If so, cut both into fine strips.

Drop the green onion into a bowl of cold water for a few seconds for the strips to curl. Keep lifting out so they don't curl too tightly. Avoid using iced water as the green onions will frizz like a tight perm. Use to garnish salads, barbecued meats, oriental dishes and buffet platters of meats.

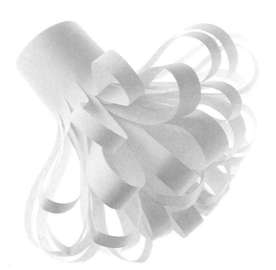

HAM OR CHOP FRILLS

Take a rectangular sheet of white paper and fold over so the longer sides meet. Avoid creasing the folded edge. With scissors, make cuts along the folded edge of the paper but do not cut all the way through.

Make the cuts in the paper close together until the end is reached, then open the paper flat, turn it over and fold again so that the longer sides of the paper meet. Turning the paper inside out gives the edge a frilly effect.

The paper frill is rolled around the bone on a leg of ham and the end of the paper is secured with tape. The frill adds a festive touch and is also used to help the carver grip the leg. Tiny frills made the same way using small rectangles of paper are used for garnishing chops, crown-rib roasts and chicken drumsticks.

CELERY CURLS

Celery curls, a favorite garnish, are used for all salads, meat platters, seafood dishes and dips. Separate the celery stalks from the base, wash well and cut into finger lengths. Split each piece in half lengthwise.

Make parallel lengthwise cuts in the celery, close together and almost to the end leaving about one-quarter of the length intact. Use a fine-bladed, sharp vegetable knife for best results.

Drop the celery into iced water and leave chilled for several hours or overnight until they open out. Drain and shake dry before using. Another way to curl the celery is to make cuts in each end, leaving the center uncut.

GRAPE GARNISHES

Grape Flower: Grapes are a natural garnish. They add color and appeal to party platters, savory and sweet dishes and are often used in salads. For grape flowers, cut a large green grape lengthwise into 4, taking care not to cut all the way through and place a maraschino cherry in the center.

Grape Fan: Grape fans are made by slicing each large unseeded grape lengthwise, making 6 or 7 slices and taking care not to cut all the way through to the stem end. Gently press out into a fan shape. Use in salads or for decorating fruit tarts and cakes.

Peeled Grapes: Peeled grapes are used for classic dishes such as Sole Véronique and also chicken. The preparation is time consuming, but the result is well worth the effort. Choose large green grapes and, using a small sharp knife, peel away the skin.

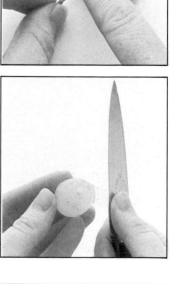

————— PINEAPPLE CRADLES —————

Remove the top from a pineapple and, holding the fruit upright, cut a thick lengthwise slice, avoiding the center core. Lay the slice of pineapple skin-side down and trim away the end. Cut into 2-inch-wide pieces.

Slice the skin from the sides of the piece of pineapple, leaving the underneath skin attached. Using a small vegetable knife, cut down ½ inch from the side of the pineapple, then underneath and back up the other side.

Lift the center pineapple flesh out, leaving a shell. Slice the pineapple flesh and arrange slices in the cradle, adding other fruit, like sliced tamarillo. Some of the green top can be trimmed and used to garnish the cradle. Serve with other fruits for dessert or as part of a buffet spread.

PEAR FANS

An elegant way of serving poached pears for dessert. Peel pears and cut into halves lengthwise. Using a melon baller or a teaspoon, scoop out the seeds. Make a syrup of 2 cups water or 1 cup water and 1 cup white wine and ½ cup sugar. Drop pears into the syrup.

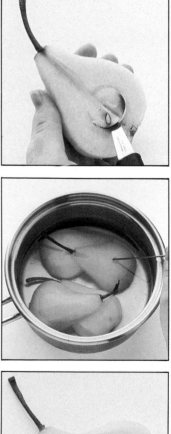

If cooking many pears, poach in 2 or 3 batches. Return the syrup to a boil; reduce heat and poach pears gently until tender. Ripe fruit needs only 8 minutes while underripe fruit will take longer. Test with a skewer. Allow pears to cool in the syrup.

Cut each pear half into about 10 slices, leaving the top of the pear uncut. Place on individual serving dishes and gently press with fingers so the pear naturally fans out. The syrup may be boiled until reduced, then cooled and a little spooned over each pear.

GUAVA CUPS

This method of cutting fruit is called *Van Dyke*. Melons, lemons, limes, oranges and tomatoes are often presented this way. Make V-shaped cuts all the way around the fruit, cutting through to the center of the fruit.

When the guava is cut all the way around, gently separate the 2 sections by holding the fruit in both hands and easing apart. Use for fruit platters and for desserts. Tomatoes can be filled with rice or potato salad or topped with herb and garlic breadcrumbs and baked to serve as an accompaniment to meals.

Another way to cut this pattern is to make a deep vertical cut in the guava, followed by an angled cut, then another straight cut. Continue all the way around the fruit and separate in the same way. A few strips of lime peel may decorate the center of the guava.

MELON BASKETS

Use a round coin and hold against the skin of a melon to mark a scalloped patter with a fine skewer. Repeat all the way around the melon. This can be done in the center of the melon or, for larger fruit, towards the stem end the process repeated at the other end to make 2 scalloped cups.

With a fine-bladed, sharp knife, cut the melon into scallops following the pattern. Make sure the cuts go right through the skin and flesh. Holding the melon in both hands separate the 2 halves. Discard the seeds.

Using a melon baller, scoop flesh from melons. A mixture of honeydew and cantaloupe can be used with a few berries. A large watermelon cut this way makes a festive centerpiece for a party table. Smaller melons can be grouped together or served individually as dessert.

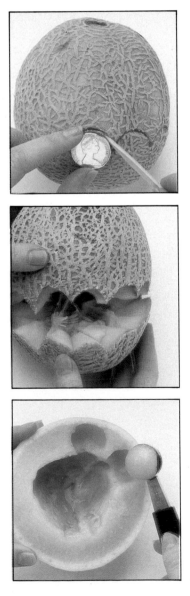

CITRUS SEGMENTS

Segments of citrus fruit are used in fruit desserts or in salads, such as orange, onion and black olive salad, drizzled with a little French dressing, to accompany duck. The fruits are peeled thickly so the skin and all the white pith are removed.

Make a cut into the orange, slicing very close to the membrane of one of the segments. Once the center of the orange is reached, twist the knife so the segment will lift out. Repeat all the way around the orange.

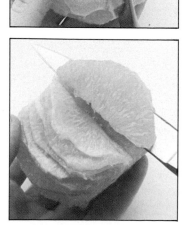

Grapefruit may also be prepared this way making an excellent starter for breakfast or a main meal, or for use in salads. Once all the fruit has been removed, squeeze any juice from the remaining membranes over the fruit.

LIME WEDGES

Lemons or oranges may be cut the same way for this versatile garnish. Use for decorating cakes and desserts or to top pâtés, mousses and seafood dishes. Halve a lime lengthwise from the stem to the base.

Lay the lime cut-side down and make a small cut near the center, angling the knife. Make another cut so a wedge can be removed from the lime. It is essential to use a very sharp knife.

Continue to cut the lime, following the lines of the first cut and removing each wedge-shaped slice as it is cut. The remaining lime can be used for cooking or in drinks.

——— MANGO HEDGEHOGS ———

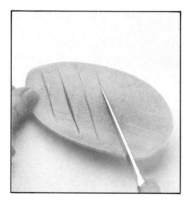

Slice off the 2 fleshy cheeks from the mango, cutting close to the seed. Place one cheek, skin-side down, on a surface and cut the flesh into evenly spaced diagonal lines, taking care not to sever the skin.

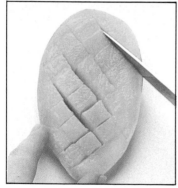

Cut the flesh of the mango cheek in the opposite direction making more evenly spaced diagonal lines so the cuts form a diamond pattern. Repeat the diagonal cuts with the other mango cheek.

Hold the cut mango in both hands and ease upward so the shape is reversed and the cuts spread out. Serve as an addition to fruit platters or as a garnish to meat platters and exotic curries. Pictured with the mango is sliced tamarillo and mint.

STAR & PASSION FRUIT

Many fruits are an attractive garnish by themselves. The tropical starfruit is simply sliced to decorate cakes, tartlets and fruit flans or it is mixed with other fruits for compotes and fresh salads.

Passion fruit can be cut *Van Dyke* style, page 86, to serve with other fruits. Using a small sharp knife, make zigzag cuts all the way around the fruit, cutting through the hard skin.

Pull the 2 halves of the fruit apart. Make lots of passion fruit cups when in season and serve on ice. A delicious finale to summer luncheons, especially when accompanied by wedges of melon. Simply serve the passion fruit with a small spoon.

—————— STRAWBERRY FANS ——————

Choose firm, ripe, red strawberries. Place strawberry, hull down, on a board and make cuts in the berry, taking care not to slice all the way through. The number of cuts depends on the size of the strawberry – 4 for small berries and 8 for larger ones.

Hold the strawberry gently and twist in the opposite direction so that the slices fan out. With the point of a knife carefully cut out the green hull.

Kumquats also make an effective garnish when prepared in this way, particularly when the oval-shaped fruit is available.

Replace the hull with a sprig of fresh mint. These fanned strawberries look attractive as a decoration for desserts and cakes. They give first courses and salads that added touch, particularly when served with smoked turkey or trout.

———— LIME CAMELLIAS ————

Oranges and lemons can be prepared in the same way to garnish salads, seafood dishes and desserts. Halve the lime lengthwise and place cut-side down on a board. Using a very sharp knife, slice the lime thinly.

Before starting to make the flower, have ready some fine wooden picks and break into short pieces. Take a lime slice from the smaller end of the fruit and curl the slice around to form the center of the camellia garnish.

The secret in making the flower is to work upside down. Place the center curl skin-side down and wrap a lime slice around it. Add another slice, overlapping the first and repeat until there are enough slices to form a manageable flower. Secure with wooden picks and gently turn over the delicate lime camellia.

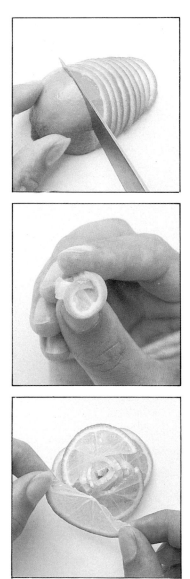

HONEYDEW WEDGES

An interesting way to serve melon wedges for a fruit platter and desserts. Cut a honeydew or cantaloupe melon into wedges and remove the seeds. Take one wedge of the melon and, using a sharp knife, mark a line ¼ inch inside the cut edge all around the skin. Following the marked line, cut through the skin.

Lay the melon wedge skin-side down and slice the flesh away from the skin, cutting three-quarters along the wedge so the top quarter is still intact. The cut-out pattern in the skin will lift out easily.

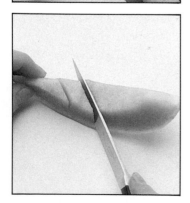

Another way to serve the melon is to cut it into wedges and remove the seeds. Cut the flesh of each melon wedge at an angle through to the skin making several evenly spaced cuts. The flesh can be separated from the skin but leave it in position.

─── MELON FANS ───

These interesting melon shapes could be used to garnish many dishes, acting as dividers or borders to both sweet and savory meals. Halve a cantaloupe melon lengthwise and scoop out the seeds. Cut the melon into thick slices and peel away the skin.

Starting at the edge of the melon slice, make a straight cut parallel to the edge and slicing three-quarters of the way down. About ½ inch further along, make a slanted diagonal cut until the first cut is reached and remove the wedge of melon.

Continue to cut the melon this way until the end is reached. Repeat with the other melon slices. Honeydew or cantaloupe melon cut this way and served with folds of prosciutto gives the popular Italian dish a new look.

APPLE BOATS

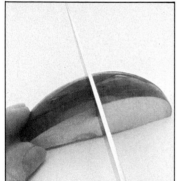

Halve an apple from stem to base and lay cut-side down. Use a fine-bladed, very sharp knife and make 2 diagonal cuts in the center of the apple, angling the knife to form a small wedge. Remove the wedge and set aside.

Following the lines of the first wedge on the apple half, cut out 4 more wedges, each one larger than the one before. Reshape the 4 smallest wedges and cut directly across into halves.

Replace the cut wedges in the remaining largest wedge and gently spread out one end to give a layered effect. Repeat with the other end. The apples will discolor if prepared too far in advance. Dip in lemon juice to prevent discoloration, if desired. Use in fruit platters.

APPLE WINGS

Divide a red eating apple evenly into 6 wedges. Use a small sharp knife to mark a triangular piece at the base of the apple wedge, penetrating the skin only. Peel away the triangular shaped piece of skin.

Carefully cut the skin away from the apple flesh, starting at the pointed end. Leave about 1 inch of skin attached at the other end. The apples are used in fruit platters for desserts. They can be served like this or cut out as described below.

Using the point of a very sharp knife, mark an outline ¼ inch from the edge of the apple, leaving a wide strip of skin in the center of the apple. Lift out the 2 center pieces of the wing, leaving the pattern as shown in the top photograph.

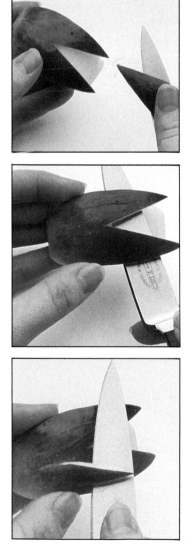

——— ORANGE STRIPS ———

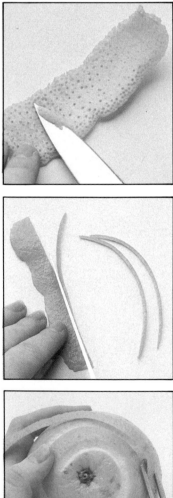

Fine slivers of orange peel cooked in a sugar syrup are an excellent garnish for desserts and add flavor when cooked with fruit, such as pear or apple. Cut the peel from oranges using a vegetable peeler. Scrape away any of the white pith which is bitter to eat.

Cut the pieces of peel into fine strips with a sharp knife and simmer in a syrup made with ½ cup sugar and 1 cup water until the peel is tender, about 5 minutes. For soups, such as borsch, simmer the orange peel in plain water and drain before adding to the soup.

To make an orange coil, use a grooved citrus zester and cut a strip of peel around the orange until there is a long strip. Drop into the syrup and simmer 5 minutes. Drain and use to decorate ice cream, fruit desserts, drinks or float in a bowl of punch.

SPUN SUGAR

Put 2 cups sugar and ½ cup water into a saucepan; stir over low heat until sugar dissolves. Wash down the inside of the saucepan with a brush dipped in water to remove any sugar crystals. Bring the syrup to a boil. When beginning to color, drop a little of the syrup into cold water. If it hardens almost immediately, the syrup is ready.

Sit the saucepan in the sink containing a little cold water to avoid further cooking. Dip a fork into the syrup and lift up so a fine thread of the sugar runs from the fork. It may be necessary to do this several times until the syrup has cooled to the correct temperature.

Run the threads of sugar from the fork onto the cake or dessert or on a sheet of parchment paper or foil. Twirl the fork around in circles until a light pile of spun sugar is formed. The sugar must be spun just before serving as it quickly dissolves, particularly when the weather is humid.

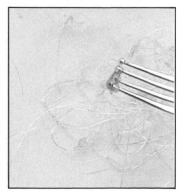

WAXED ROSES

Paraffin wax gives flowers a soft appearance and helps keep them longer. A bunch of white waxed roses with satin ribbon is a lovely decoration for wedding cakes. Trim the roses, leaving enough stem for holding. Keep some of the leaves for waxing also.

Melt the paraffin wax in a saucepan over very low heat. Test the temperature with the leaves. Dip into the wax; if it sizzles, the wax is too hot and will bruise the roses. When the wax no longer sizzles, dip several leaves, one at a time, in the wax and leave to set.

Dip the roses, one at a time, in the wax and leave to set. If the wax sets before all the roses are dipped, warm gently and test again with a leaf before waxing another flower. Trim off the stem to the desired length and use to decorate cakes and desserts. Other flowers may be waxed in the same way.

SUGARED FLOWERS

Beat an egg white with a fork until just mixed but not frothy. Use a fine brush to paint the egg white onto the flowers, coating both the front and back of violets or sweet peas. Rose petals and other edible flowers can be prepared in the same way.

As each flower is coated with the egg white, place on a sheet of paper thickly coated with superfine sugar. Sprinkle more sugar over the top. If any parts are not coated, gently dab on more egg white and sprinkle with a little more sugar.

As each flower is sugared, place on a rack in an airy place to dry. If the weather is damp, place the sugared flowers on a baking sheet in a 300F (150C) oven 10 minutes. Remove; cool. Use to decorate cakes, desserts and homemade chocolates.

CRIMPED PASTRY

Edgings on tarts not only give an attractive finish, they also seal the pastry together when used for filled pies. Use a shortcrust or pie pastry and roll out thinly. Line a pie plate with the pastry.

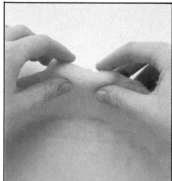

Trim the pastry, leaving enough overhang to tuck under, forming a thicker edge for crimping a pattern. Gently press the pastry rim to make an even thickness all the way around.

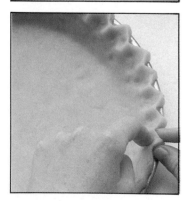

Place the index finger of one hand on the inside of the pastry rim and, using the index finger and thumb of the other hand, pinch the pastry to a point. Repeat all the way around. If necessary, dust fingers in a little flour to prevent sticking. Chill before baking.

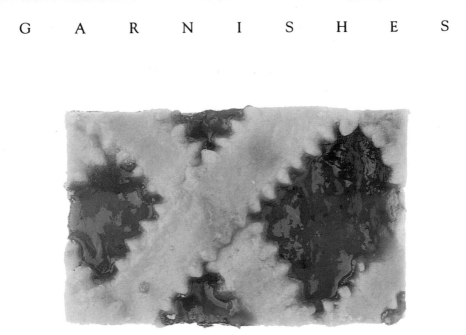

LATTICE PASTRY

Use a sweet shortcrust or a pie pastry and roll out to an oblong shape. Place on a greased baking sheet. Roll out more pastry and cut into strips with a pastry wheel, using a ruler to keep the strips straight.

Spread the first sheet of pastry with jam and place one of the strips diagonally over the jam-topped pastry. Add another strip in the opposite direction. Add another strip parallel to the first.

More strips are placed on the jam topped pastry, one at a time, weaving the pastry over and under. Trim edges and bake in a 400F (200F) oven until golden. The lattice pastry may be used for fruit pies.

SUGARED GRAPES

Choose green, dark or wine-colored grapes or a mixture of all of these for sugar coating. Use to decorate cakes, desserts and sweet tarts. Wash the grapes well and dry thoroughly, then snip into small clusters with scissors.

Beat an egg white with a fork to mix until just beginning to form a few bubbles. Use a fine brush to paint the egg white onto the grapes. Make sure the grapes are thoroughly and evenly coated with egg white.

Place the cluster of grapes on a sheet of waxed paper, dusted thickly with superfine sugar. Using a fine sieve, thickly dust more sugar over the grapes. Shake off the excess sugar and place the grapes on a rack to dry.

SHORTBREAD HEARTS

Cream together ½ cup butter, ⅓ cup sugar and ½ teaspoon vanilla extract. Add 1 cup all-purpose flour and ½ cup self-raising flour. Shape into a ball of dough. Cover and rest 30 minutes. Roll out dough ¼-inch thick between 2 sheets of plastic wrap.

Cut out with a heart-shaped cutter. Place on baking sheets and bake at 350F (180C) 10 minutes or until hearts are pale and golden in color. Trimmings can be gathered and rolled again.

Remove immediately from trays onto a rack and dust with powdered sugar. Leave cool. Then, store in an airtight container. Serve with desserts, such as fresh raspberries or strawberries. Makes 12 to 15.

GLAZED FRUIT TARTS

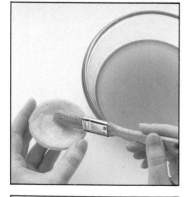

A fruit glaze brushed over fruit tarts enhances the color and appeal. For light-colored fruits, such as apricots, gooseberries and grapes, use an apricot jam, and for red fruits, such as strawberries, use a red currant jelly. Spoon 1 cup jam or jelly into a saucepan. Add 2 tablespoons brandy and a squeeze of lemon juice.

Heat, stirring jam until smooth. Simmer 5 minutes. Strain through a nylon sieve. Cool and brush onto the insides of cooked tartlet pastry or a large flan pastry.

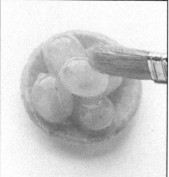

Arrange fruit in the tart pastry and brush with the glaze. Allow to set before serving. The glaze can be kept in a covered jar in the refrigerator for several months. Fruits on top of cheesecakes and flan pastry are given an appealing gloss when brushed with the glaze.

——— APPLE CAGES ———

Peel cooking apples and remove cores. Make a syrup of 3 cups water and 1 cup granulated sugar. Stir until sugar dissolves; then bring to a boil. Add apples; poach over low heat until apples are tender, 10 to 20 minutes. Lift apples out of the syrup and leave cool.

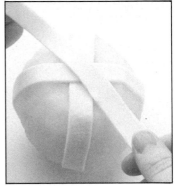

Cut sheets of purchased puff pastry into strips. If pastry is frozen, thaw slightly before cutting. Allow 4 strips for each apple. Place 1 strip around each apple, tucking in the ends. Place another strip across the first strip and tuck underneath. Cross remaining 2 strips of pastry over the apple at even intervals. Cut leaves from pastry and place on each apple.

Brush the pastry on apples with beaten egg and sprinkle with a little granulated sugar. Bake on greased baking sheets in a preheated 400F (200C) oven 15 minutes or until pastry is golden. Meanwhile, boil the syrup until slightly reduced and spoon a little around each apple.

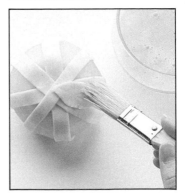

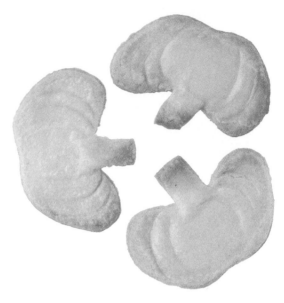

PASTRY PUMPKINS

Pastry decorations give pies and flans a special finish. These little pumpkins look equally good for apple pies. Use a plain round cookie cutter and press the edge so one side is well dented (for the top) and the opposite side has a slight dent (base).

Roll out pastry trimmings from shortcrust or pie pastry ¼-inch thick between 2 sheets of plastic wrap. Remove top sheet of plastic and cut pastry into pumpkin shapes. Place on greased baking sheets.

Using the edge of the cutter, make 2 or 3 markings on the pumpkin shape to resemble the real vegetable. Cut out small oblong shapes for the stalks and press on the pastry. Brush with beaten egg and bake in a 375F (190C) oven until golden. Cool.

PUFF PASTRY ROSES

Sheets of frozen puff pastry are ideal for topping meat casseroles. Roses and leaves add a special touch. To make a rose, cut a strip of the pastry and fold one end over to start the center of the flower.

Wrap the strip of pastry around the centre, occasionally pinching a crease in the pastry to give a fuller open effect. When the rose or bud is the required size, place on a greased baking sheet and brush with beaten egg to glaze. Bake in a 200C (400F/gas 6) oven 10 minutes or until golden.

Leaves are made by cutting shapes out of the pastry and marking the veins with a knife. Bake the same way as the roses. Alternatively, roses and leaves may be placed on the uncooked pie, glazed with egg and baked as described in the recipe. Traditionally, savory pies are decorated while fruit pies are left plain.

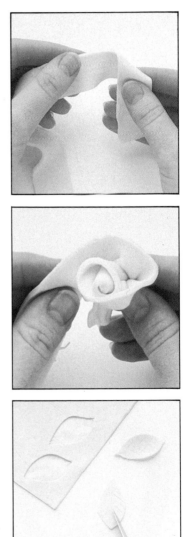

———— CHOCOLATE BOXES ————

Made with square chocolate mints, these little chocolate boxes make a delightful dessert. Cut plain cake into squares the same size as the chocolate mints. Cut each square of cake into ½ inch slices. Homemade butter cake or a bought plain cake can be used.

Warm a little strawberry jam or red currant jelly with a dash of brandy, orange liqueur or port. Cool slightly and spread over the sides and top of cake squares, leaving the underside unglazed.

Whip cream until thickened; just before serving, spread over each jam-glazed square of cake, covering the top and sides. Place 4 chocolate mints around each cake and place each on a serving plate. Decorate with strawberry fans, page 92, or sugared flowers, page 101.

CHOCOLATE CUPS

These chocolate cups can be filled with liqueurs or flavored cream and topped with a berry to serve with coffee. Melt semisweet chocolate over hot, not boiling, water. Use a brush to paint the chocolate on the inside of foil cases, making sure the top edge is fairly thick.

Leave the cups in a cool place to set. During hot weather, put into freezer briefly and remove once the chocolate has firmed. Peel away the foil cups, using a skewer to separate the chocolate from the foil.

A colorful decoration for the cups are chocolate-joined nasturtium leaves. Separate the petals from the flowers and join by brushing the tips with melted chocolate. Leave set and place on the cream filled cups. Rose petals may be done the same way.

COOKIE CUPS

Cream together 6 tablespoons butter and sugar until light. Beat in 2 egg whites, one at a time; then stir in 3 tablespoons all-purpose flour until mixed. Drop 1 tablespoon mixture onto a baking sheet lined with parchment paper.

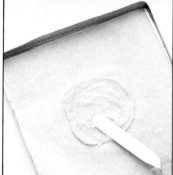

Make one cup at a time. Spread each out thinly with a spatula and bake at 350F (180C) 3 to 10 minutes or until golden. With practice, 2 or 3 can be made at a time.

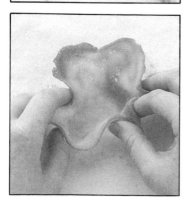

Cool the cookie rounds slightly; while still warm lift from the paper and shape with fingers into fluted cups. If the cookie cools and becomes crisp before the shape is set, return to the oven and repeat. Store airtight and use for serving desserts, filling the cups with ice cream, fruit and cream desserts. Makes about 6.

—— COOKIE BUTTERFLY ——

Make the cookie mixture as described on the opposite page. Draw butterfly wings on sheets of parchment paper and place, upside down, on baking sheets so the cookie mixture does not contact the lead tracings.

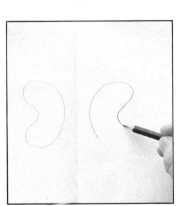

Spread cookie mixture thinly, keeping within the outline of the butterfly wings, making sure it spreads evenly. Bake in a 350F (180C) oven until golden around the edges. Lift off paper and cool on racks.

Melt semisweet chocolate in a bowl over hot, not boiling, water. Add a few drips of cold water to thicken the chocolate. Spoon into a piping bag and pipe a butterfly body onto parchment paper or foil. Place the wings into position and leave to set. If needed, pipe a little chocolate under the wings to give support. Use to decorate ice cream and other desserts. Makes 8 to 10.

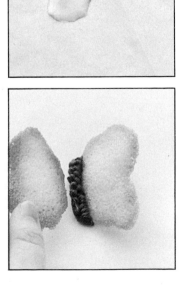

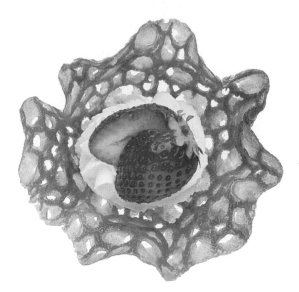

—— BRANDY SNAP BASKETS ——

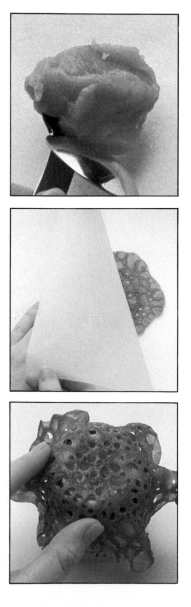

In a medium saucepan, combine ¼ cup butter, ½ cup superfine sugar, 1 teaspoon ground ginger and ⅓ cup light corn syrup. Heat gently until butter melts. Cool and stir in ½ cup all-purpose flour. Drop a heaping teaspoonful onto a parchment-lined baking sheet.

Bake in a preheated 350F (180C) oven 10 minutes or until the cookie begins to darken around the edge. Cool a few seconds, then turn paper upside down and peel away from the cookie. The parchment paper can be used again.

Working quickly before the cookie sets, pick it up and mold over an upturned cup or mold, fluting out the edge. If the cookie hardens before the cup is formed, return to the oven to soften. Just before serving, fill with cream, ice cream and fruits. Lemon Soufflé is a particularly good filling for the brandy snap baskets. Makes 6 to 8.

CHOCOLATE COATINGS

Chocolate Leaves: Chop dark unsweetened or semisweet chocolate. Melt in a bowl over hot, not boiling, water. Choose non-poisonous leaves, such as camellia or rose; wipe with paper towels. Use a small brush to brush the leaves with melted chocolate. When set, peel away the leaf. Use leaves to decorate desserts and cakes.

Chocolate-dipped Strawberries: Dip strawberries into melted chocolate so the coating is halfway up the side of the berry. Allow excess chocolate to drip off; leave to set on foil-lined trays. Serve with after-dinner coffee or use to decorate cakes and desserts.

Chocolate Coating: Chocolate is used to coat crisp nut cookies, such as the famous Florentines, which are delicious served with coffee. Spread the melted chocolate on the back of the cookies. Using a metal icing comb, make "waves" in the chocolate.

CHOCOLATE CURLS

Chop semisweet chocolate; put into a clean bowl over a pan of warm water to melt. If the water is too hot, the chocolate will be flecked with light spots.

Do not allow one drop of water to mix into the chocolate as this will make it thick and impossible to curl. Pour the chocolate onto a slab, preferably marble, and spread evenly. Keep working the spatula backward and forward until the chocolate firms.

As soon as the chocolate sets, form into curls using a very sharp knife or a cheese cutter. Use chocolate curls to decorate cakes and desserts. Any chocolate that remains on the slab can be scraped up and used again.

CHOCOLATE SHAPES

To make a paper piping bag, cut a triangle of waxed paper. Holding one corner in your right hand, roll over to form a sharp point in the longer side of the triangle. Wrap the paper around and tuck in the top to secure.

Chocolate Lattice: Half-fill the piping bag with melted dark chocolate. Snip the point of the bag for the chocolate to flow. Line baking sheets with parchment paper or foil and pipe lattice shapes on the paper. Leave to set. Peel off and use to top ice-cream desserts.

Chocolate Flower: Make sure there is a thick dot of chocolate in the center (the weakest point) to hold the flower together. Pipe 5 petal shapes around it. Use for desserts or on top of iced cakes.

──── CAKE STENCILS ────

This easy cake decoration is very effective for sponge cakes and rich chocolate cakes. Cut strips of waxed paper and lay on the cake, some at angles. Sift powdered sugar over and carefully lift off the paper.

Paper doilies give round cakes an interesting finish. Place the doily on the cake and dust powdered sugar thickly through a sieve. For children's party cakes, animal shapes can be cut out of waxed paper and placed on the cake before powdered sugar is sifted over.

Lift off the paper doily leaving sugar decoration on the cake. With a little imagination, many messages and designs can be cut out of paper for cakes decorated this way.

—— FINISHING TOUCHES ——

Scorched Sugar: Powdered-sugar-coated desserts, such as puff pastry fingers and soufflé omelets are given a professional touch when a hot skewer caramelizes the coating. Heat the skewer over a flame until red hot; then place it on the sugar-coated dessert. When brown, make another parallel stripe. Reheat the skewer when necessary.

Chocolate Piping: Iced tarts or cakes are finished with a simple chocolate piping. Melt chopped chocolate over warm, not hot, water and spoon into a piping bag. Pipe double lines on the iced tart.

Praline: A delicious decoration for most desserts from ice cream to fruit. The caramel almonds can be bought or made with your favorite recipe. Place the sugar-coated almonds into a plastic bag and crush with a rolling pin to a powder. Store airtight.

ICING NUMBERS

Make Royal Icing by stirring 1 egg white with fork until foamy. Sift 1½ cups powdered sugar and gradually beat into the white. Add more sifted powdered sugar if necessary to make a firm icing. Use a skewer to add a few drops of lemon juice. Color as desired. Keep icing closely covered with plastic wrap.

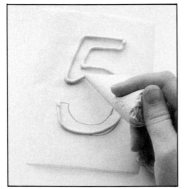

Draw a double outline of the number, marking it clearly in thick pencil on a piece of waxed paper and turn the paper over. Trace the number on a piece of parchment paper and turn over (it's done twice because it's difficult to pipe a reversed number). Make a paper icing bag (see page 117) and fill with half the icing. Snip ⅛ inch off the pointed end and pipe an outline of the number. Leave to set.

Add enough cold water to the remaining icing so that it falls in a steady stream from a spoon. Fill another bag with this icing mixture and allow the icing to run within the lines of the number. Leave until set. Lift the number off the paper and use to decorate birthday cakes. The numbers can be made weeks in advance and stored in airtight containers.

MERINGUE MUSHROOMS

Sift 1 cup superfine sugar on to a sheet of paper. Whisk 3 egg whites with a pinch of cream of tartar until soft peaks form when the beaters are lifted. Gradually beat in 2 rounded tablespoons of the sugar. Add remaining sugar all at once and carefully fold into the egg whites.

Use parchment paper on baking sheets or brush the sheets with oil and sift a little all-purpose flour over. Tap off excess flour. Place meringue in piping bag. Pipe the stems of the mushrooms by squeezing a little meringue mixture on the sheet lifting to a peak. Squeeze out small rounds for the mushroom caps.

Dust the caps of the mushrooms with unsweetened cocoa powder pushed through a fine sieve. Bake the meringues in a 300F (150C) oven for 1 hour or until meringues are dry. Turn the meringues over, turn off oven and leave meringues in oven until cool. Join the stems to the caps with a little icing or cream. Serve as petits fours or on top of cakes for decoration. Makes about 24.

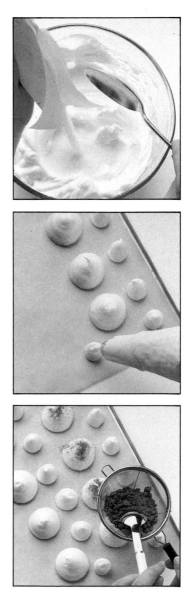

FEATHER ICING

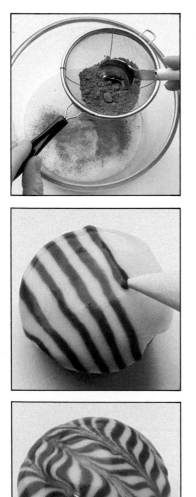

A striking pattern for large or small iced cakes or tarts which can be made in any color. Sift 1½ cups powdered sugar; stir in 1½ tablespoons boiling water. Icing should be thick but run freely from the spoon. Put half the icing in another bowl; sift in 2 teaspoons unsweetened cocoa powder and add a little more water. Both icings should be the same consistency.

Spread the white icing over the cake. For large cakes, tie a band of waxed paper around cake to avoid icing running down the sides. Put the chocolate icing into a piping bag and pipe straight lines across the white icing. The secret is to not allow the icing to set before the decoration is complete.

While the icing is still wet, draw a skewer through the lines, running in opposite directions. When the first line is completed, turn cake around and draw the skewer in the opposite direction to the first to achieve the feathered pattern.

—— ORANGE CARTWHEELS ——

Without the chocolate, orange cartwheels are effective for decorating drinks
and salad platters. With the chocolate,
they make a good partner for coffee or
cold desserts. Use a citrus grooving tool
to make a pattern in the peel of the
orange, spacing the grooves around the
orange as evenly as possible.

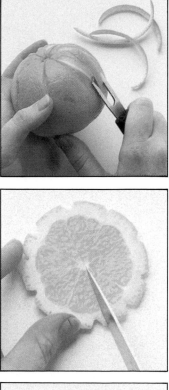

Slice the orange in the usual way. For
drinks, make a cut from the outside edge
to the middle of the orange slice and slip
over the rim of a glass. The orange may
be twisted by holding the two points of
the cut and twisting in opposite directions. Use to garnish salads and duck
and meat dishes.

To make the chocolate cartwheels, chop
dark chocolate and melt in a bowl over
hot, not boiling, water. Spoon a little in
the center of the slice of orange and
spread with the back of a teaspoon.
Allow to set. The orange slices may be
cut into halves for easier serving.

SAVORY GARNISHES

Lobster Medallions with Lobster Butterfly, page 25; Lemon Swan, page 31, and Julienne of Vegetables, page 26.

Butterfly Shrimp, page 47, with Cucumber Borders, page 76, and Lemon Twist, page 44.

Fried Fish with Chili Wild Flowers, page 11, and Lime Wedges, page 89.

Asian Salad with Lotus Flower, page 64; Red-Pepper Triangles, page 53; and Edible Pea Pods, page 24.

Grilled Steak with Fluted Mushrooms, page 41; Bean Bundles, page 33.

Roast Duck with Orange Strips, page 98; Carrot Curls, page 56; and Orange Segments, page 88.

Raspberries and Cream with Shortbread Hearts, page 105.

Sponge Cake with Feather Icing, page 122.

Clockwise from top: Guava Cups, page 86; Starfruit, page 91; Sliced Tamarillo, Melon Fan, page 95; Apple Boat, Page 96; and Mango Hedgehog, page 90.

Ice cream in Brandy Snap Basket, page 114, with Orange Strips, page 98, and Chocolate Lattice, page 117.

INDEX